Class 66.

MARK V. PIKE

KEY
Books

BRITAIN'S RAILWAYS SERIES, VOLUME 32

Front cover image: 66120 with 66171 (on the rear) are seen exiting Buckhorn Weston Tunnel, just west of Gillingham, Dorset, with 6N01, the 07.42 Yeovil Junction to Eastleigh Yard ballast train, rarely routed direct to Salisbury and not, as is usually the case, via Westbury. Hard to imagine now, but this was once a double track main line throughout. 4 May 2014.

Back cover image: An immaculate 66077 *Benjamin Gimbert GC* departs Eastleigh with 4O43, the 03.59 Wakefield to Southampton Western Docks. 2 October 2019.

Title page image: Conveniently parked at the former Godfrey Road stabling point at Newport, 66185+66204+66166 make for an interesting image. Only 66185 is still working in the UK at the time of writing, now in DB red livery and named *DP World London Gateway*. 25 July 2001.

Contents page image: Various detail differences can be seen here as the first and last locos of the EWS order are seen side by side. 66001 and 66250 are on display at the Old Oak Common open day. 1 August 2000.

Published by Key Books
An imprint of Key Publishing Ltd
PO Box 100
Stamford
Lincs PE19 1XQ

www.keypublishing.com

The rights of Mark V. Pike to be identified as the author of this book has been asserted in accordance with the Copyright, Designs and Patents Act 1988 Sections 77 and 78.

Copyright © Mark V. Pike, 2022

ISBN 978 1 80282 254 0

Typeset by SJmagic DESIGN SERVICES, India.

Contents

Introduction

The English, Welsh & Scottish Railway (EWS) freight company was formed in the UK in 1996, and hot on the heels of this development came an order for 250 locomotives with General Motors that were similar in design to the already proven Class 59. The arrival of the EWS Class 66 locomotives is perhaps infamously remembered by rail enthusiasts as a death knell for many of the well-known and loved examples of British diesel traction then in service. However, EWS was not created to cater for enthusiasts, and for the people more interested in the future of freight on the railways, the introduction of the Class 66s was greeted with a little more joy!

Up to this time, the introduction of any sort of new rolling stock in the UK, especially locomotives, was always a long and drawn-out process. However, much of this was avoided by using the Class 59s as a basis, allowing the Class 66s to be delivered speedily, and indeed put into service very quickly. This obviously hastened the demise of some British types that might otherwise have remained in service for longer. This is not to say that there were no teething troubles; indeed, 66002 was held back from delivery to the UK for over a year as it was used for ironing these problems out, helping considerably when the later locos were delivered.

Now, after almost 25 years of service, the locos have proved to be well worth the £300-odd million they cost with only a few failures and no serious problems. At the present time (February 2022), it certainly looks as though they will stay around for many more years to come. This first volume of over 230 images shows the original sub-class of this now ubiquitous type at work in the UK hauling various trains.

66165 in the sidings at Southampton Up Yard. 15 February 2018.

Chapter 1
General Freight

The Class 66/0 was specifically designed for freight traffic, and this subject obviously forms the majority of this book. In this section are many workings that have been observed over the years, with a bias towards the south of the country. Many of these flows have now been lost, but there are also a fair few that still operate to this day.

Right: 66001, the doyen of the class, and still looking quite new after five years of service, approaches Southampton Central from the Freemantle footbridge with 6O41, the 10.14 Westbury to Eastleigh East Yard engineers' train. This is now a GB Railfreight (GBRf)-operated service. 4 September 2003.

Below: A few months later, and 66001 is again seen at Southampton Central with 6V41, the 14.45 Eastleigh East Yard to Westbury, the return working to that seen in the previous image, and which is also now GBRf operated. This train can often produce some unusual consists, and this time it was nothing but a small engineers' crane. 11 March 2004.

Ten years further on, and 66001 was a relatively early recipient of the DB bright red livery. It is seen just north of Southampton, this time on a damp afternoon as it approaches Mount Pleasant level crossing, near St Denys, with 4O40 the 09.43 Morris Cowley to Southampton Eastern Docks car train. 7 May 2014.

Approaching Campbell Road bridge at Eastleigh, this is 66247 with 6B62, the 09.13 Fawley to Eastleigh Yard oil train. This service has long since ceased, and the loco itself was sent to work in Europe during the mid-2000s and has been there ever since operating for DB's French subsidiary. 25 March 2004.

The winter morning sunshine nicely illuminates 66221 as it departs from Eastleigh with another long-lost service, 6W53, the 08.45 Eastleigh Yard to Furzebrook liquid petroleum gas (LPG) tanks. 18 February 2004.

A totally unrepeatable image. This is 66036 at the Godfrey Road stabling point at Newport station, which has now been obliterated beneath a new station building, an extra platform and overhead catenary. This is another loco that has since been exported to work in Europe for DB. 28 September 2004.

This time we see 66032 stabled at Westbury, not long before it too was exported to work in Europe. However, during late 2021, it was repatriated back to Toton depot and has undergone the various modifications required to allow it to work on the UK network once again. It is now in DB red livery with a return to service imminent. 9 October 2003.

Another view that is now impossible to replicate. 66100 is passing along the Great Western Main Line (GWML) at Purley-on-Thames with 6M48, the 10.34 Southampton Eastern Docks to Halewood (Jaguar cars) train. 22 September 2011.

Seven years on and the same loco is seen passing Basingstoke with 4O21, the 09.15 Trafford Park to Southampton Western Docks in spotless DB red livery. It had also recently been named *Armistice 100* in commemoration of 100 years since the end of World War One. 13 November 2018.

This is 66112 with the 6M48 Southampton Eastern Docks to Halewood again but this time at Little Langford in the Wylye Valley, between Salisbury and Warminster. It was running off its usual route via Basingstoke due to planned engineering works in the area. 29 March 2013.

Coming up the incline and framed by the high arch bridge on the approach to Swanwick station, this is 66162 with 6Y32, the 08.24 Fawley to Holybourne oil train. This is yet another train in the Southampton area that has since stopped running. The loco itself is now in DB's Maritime Transport blue customer livery and carrying the name *Maritime Intermodal Five*. It can be seen in this guise later in this volume. 23 October 2013.

At the other end of the country at Carlisle, this is 66198 approaching the station with an unidentified long welded rail train coming off the line from Workington and the Cumbrian coast. 2 February 2004.

Above: 66064, another one of the locos currently working in Europe, is seen approaching Carlisle station with a rake of empty four-wheeled coal hoppers heading north. 1 January 2004.

Left: With a light dusting of snow on the ground, 66011 is engaged in a spot of shunting in the yard at Aberdeen with the pipes destined for use by the North Sea oil industry. 3 February 2004.

Back in the south of England, 66002 (formerly *Lafarge Quorn*) passes Salisbury with 6V41, the 14.45 Eastleigh to Westbury engineers' train. After its construction in 1998, this loco was used extensively by General Motors in Colorado, US, as a test bed for modifications. Its delivery to the UK was delayed for about a year because of this. 10 June 2016.

We now see the changing appearance of 66005 over the years, firstly passing Kensington Olympia with a northbound steel train from Dollands Moor. 19 July 2006.

Almost 13 years later, 66005 is now carrying Maritime Transport blue and named *Maritime Intermodal One* as it passes Basingstoke with 4O43, the 03.59 Wakefield Europort to Southampton Western Docks. 10 April 2019.

Lafarge
Quorn

Still at the time carrying its nameplates, being one of just a few named by EWS in the type's early years, 66002 *Lafarge Quorn* is seen again, this time approaching Westbury station with 6V18, the 12.35 Hither Green to Whatley Quarry empty stone train. While the vast majority of the fleet are nameless, strangely this loco has carried two names in its career, firstly in 2002 it was *Lafarge Buddon Wood*, but this was removed after about six months and reaffixed to 66042. This loco then became *Lafarge Quorn* in 2003 until it was removed during the 2010s at some point. With another 240 odd locos to choose from, it seems a little odd to have de-named and then re-named a loco. 1 March 2012.

Despite the sizeable Mendip contract transferring to Freightliner at the end of 2019, DB Cargo, which previously held this contract, still controls the yards at Westbury and provides main line locos for shunting purposes. This is 66096 doing the honours on a bright early spring morning. 30 March 2021.

With the revised headlight arrangement that is gradually being fitted to the class, this is 66003 (effectively the first production loco) waiting time at Clapham Junction with 7O02, the 13.06 Acton to Tolworth stone train, another service that has since passed to Freightliner. 17 June 2019.

Another one of the few locos that were named by EWS, this is 66042 *Lafarge Buddon Wood* (the name removed from 66002) powering towards Winchester with a short 6M44, the 13.31 Eastleigh Yard to Wembley 'Enterprise' service, which was discontinued in 2010. This loco is currently at work in France for DB Cargo. 15 May 2003.

This is 66134 passing through Doncaster with an early running 4L45, the 10.04 Wakefield Europort to Felixstowe South intermodal. This loco has since received DB red livery. 23 September 2015.

Still at Doncaster, and with another loco that is currently working in Europe, 66231 approaches with an unidentified southbound steel train. 29 August 2001.

Further north, 66004 is captured during a crew change at York with an unidentified southbound hopper train. This loco underwent an eye-catching transformation in 2021. It is now decked out in a one-off light green livery, emblazoned with various embellishments and with the legend 'I am a Climate Hero'. The loco can apparently only run on Hydrotreated Vegetable Oil (HVO) fuel, which sounds a bit weird but is designed to reduce emissions. 22 February 2008.

A classic scene along the Berks and Hants line between Reading and Westbury as 66065 passes by the Kennet & Avon Canal at Crofton with 6M20, the 10.34 Whatley Quarry to St Pancras loaded stone train. This working was often easily distinguishable by the motley selection of wagons it employed. 8 April 2015.

Three years later, and 66065 has now received the DB red livery. It is seen approaching West Ealing, once again working 6M20, the 10.34 Whatley Quarry to St Pancras loaded stone. 5 July 2018.

Although these images are not the best, owing to it being a thoroughly dark and wet day, they show the exceptionally rare appearance of a Class 66 (indeed any loco) on the branch line from Brockenhurst to Lymington in Hampshire. During the early part of 2004, the whole line of around 5½ miles was completely relaid with continuously welded rails, which obviously required engineering trains. This is 66039 with a loaded ballast train standing at Lymington Town station. Note the disconnected signal to the left. 5 February 2004.

On the other end of the ballast train was 66150, which is seen being hand signalled over the main B3054 level crossing, just east of Lymington Town. It is not often you will see crossing barriers seemingly open to road traffic with a train passing through them! This loco is now in DB red livery. 5 February 2004.

PAUL MELLENEY

Looking a bit like a model on a layout, this is 66172 *Paul Melleney* on the South Western Main Line passing Micheldever, running south light engine for Eastleigh Yard. 16 April 2013.

There was a period during the mid-2010s when DB found itself short of motive power. Having sent a large number of locos abroad, this was especially the case during the autumn, when more traction was needed for the various Railhead Treatment Trains (RHTT) that operate throughout the country. For this reason, a few Class 66s were retrieved temporarily from their overseas duties and hastily reconfigured for the UK network to bolster the home fleet. This is full Euro Cargo Rail (now DB Cargo France) branded 66033, which actually ended up staying in the UK a little longer due to this shortage. It is seen at Didcot North Junction running light engine from Hinksey Yard to Didcot stabling point. 10 March 2011.

Perfectly illuminated by the slow rising winter sunshine, 66090 departs Eastleigh with a late running 6Y26, the 08.15 Eastleigh Yard to Quidhampton calcium carbonate tanks. This train ceased running the following year. 16 January 2008.

66090 *Maritime Intermodal Six* is another of the seven locos to have undergone the transformation from EWS maroon livery to Maritime Transport blue. The immaculate machine is seen once again at Eastleigh, but this time waiting to depart the station with 4M71, the 09.47 Southampton Western Docks to Birch Coppice intermodal. 4 November 2019.

Above: Three images now from Lostwithiel in deepest Cornwall. This first one sees 66086 running through the down line with a loaded clay train from Fowey Docks. The semaphore signals at this location are a nice addition to any photo. 30 August 2002.

Right: This is 66148 in the down sidings just east of the station, with a rake of china clay hoppers. This is another one of those seven locos now carrying Maritime blue and is named *Maritime Intermodal Seven*. 30 August 2002.

This time 66132 is heading through the station with an eastbound clay train for Tavistock Junction. This was one of ten Class 66s that DB sold to GBRf in late 2017 and has since become 66785 in full GBRf colours. 30 August 2002.

Moving on to the London area, we see Southern Class 377 'Electrostar' 377611 heading into London Victoria and passing above 66155 at Culvert Road (near Clapham Junction), which is leading the 4E26 07.45 Dollands Moor to Scunthorpe Redbourne Sidings steel empties. With the large amount of trains going to and from Victoria, it is reasonably easy to get shots like this. 13 December 2014.

The same train as seen in the previous image, the 4E26 07.45 Dollands Moor to Scunthorpe Redbourne Sidings, is captured again, this time passing through Kensington Olympia in the charge of 66061. 26 April 2021.

Still at Kensington Olympia on the same day, this is 66107 approaching with 6O13, the 10.32 Acton to Newhaven Marine stone train. 26 April 2021.

Above: This is 66016 approaching South Greenford with 7O97, the 11.51 Paddington Yard to Angerstein Wharf. Despite later receiving DB red livery, this is another of the ten locos now working with GBRf, having been sold by DB in 2017. It now carries the number 66781. 18 February 2015.

Right: With its passing being observed by a Freightliner employee high up on his crane, this is 66004 with a bit of a patched-up front end passing Millbrook container terminal with 6B62, the 09.13 Fawley to Eastleigh oil train. This service ceased running in 2015. 4 November 2004.

Captured amongst the trees and bushes of autumn, 66162 heads north near Mortimer, on the Basingstoke to Reading line, with 4M71, the 09.47 Southampton Western Docks to Birch Coppice intermodal service. This loco has since been painted blue and named *Maritime Intermodal Five*. 29 November 2016.

From directly above Southampton Tunnel, 66017 approaches with 6Y32, the 08.24 Fawley to Holybourne oil train. This train has long ceased to run. Unfortunately, this fine view has now become extensively overgrown. 5 September 2012.

Left: Now in the bright red DB livery, 66017 passes Eastleigh with 4M71, the 09.47 Southampton Western Docks to Birch Coppice intermodal service. 9 May 2018.

Below: An unusual perspective of 66173 as the loco is seen starting the stiff climb towards Dilton Marsh soon after departure with 6O41, the 10.14 Westbury Yard to Eastleigh Yard engineers' service. This is now one of 15 locos that DB has sent to work in Poland for DB Cargo Polska. The train it is hauling still runs at the present time, but it is now in the hands of GBRf. 21 April 2011.

Coming around the long curve on the approach to Hawkeridge Junction (Westbury) on the line from Bath and Trowbridge, this is 66012 with 6W97, the 08.00 Pilning Up Loop to Westbury empty long welded rail train. 20 August 2017.

Right: This once-fine view at South Moreton on the GWML has now been lost to electrification as we see 66008 heading east with an unidentified freight. This is another of the ten locos since sold to GBRf and has now become 66780 *The Cemex Express* in a special one-off white, blue and red livery. 7 April 2011.

Below: Another great view that has now been lost, as 66068 is seen soon after passing through West Drayton with a Theale to Acton trip working. 31 August 2012.

Just about to pass through the short tunnel at Holdenhurst Road that I was standing above, 66120 is approaching Bournemouth station with the final 6V53, the 08.45 Eastleigh Yard to Furzebrook LPG train. The last loaded train went out that evening, and very soon after all the tank wagons were quickly disposed of. The original Bournemouth East terminus station stood to the right of the picture, which was the end of a branch line from Ringwood and Christchurch. With the coming of the line from Poole in the mid-1870s and the construction of Bournemouth Central through station, the old Bournemouth East was abandoned. 15 July 2005.

Since the end of steam working on the London and South Western Railway (L&SWR) main line to the west in 1967 and the drastic rationalisation that followed, any sort of freight traffic between Salisbury, Yeovil and Exeter has been very rare, especially in daylight hours. With the lovely purple Ragged Robin's adorning the cutting slopes, 66120 with 66171 on the rear are exiting the well-known location of Buckhorn Weston Tunnel with 6N01, the 07.42 Yeovil Junction to Eastleigh Yard ballast train, this being rarely routed via Gillingham instead of Westbury. Hard to imagine now, but this was once a double track main line throughout. 4 May 2014.

An immaculate 66077 *Benjamin Gimbert GC* is seen passing Cholsey on the GWML with 4O39, the 09.43 Morris Cowley to Southampton Eastern Docks car train. 18 November 2019.

A couple of years later, 66077 *Benjamin Gimbert GC* is seen again on the same train as the previous image, this time passing Basingstoke. It now carries the slogan 'Powered by HVO – Reducing our carbon footprint'. 15 October 2021.

Still carrying the full EWS livery, 66129 is approaching Eastleigh at Campbell Road bridge with 4M71, the 09.47 Southampton Western Docks to Birch Coppice intermodal service. 13 April 2021.

This is 66009 approaching a public foot crossing just south of Southampton Airport Parkway station with 6X41, the 10.14 Westbury to Eastleigh East Yard. 27 August 2015.

Six years later, and 66009 is now carrying the DB red livery as it approaches Eastleigh with 4O43, the 03.59 Wakefield Europort to Southampton Western Docks. 13 April 2021.

Amid some fine autumn colours, 66009 is seen again from a vantage point high above Popham Tunnels at Micheldever, this time with 4M71, the 09.47 Southampton Western Docks to Birch Coppice. Apart from once being an oil depot, the area to the left of the picture was also used for the storage of old coaching stock during the late 1960s and 1970s. 22 October 2018.

With a few loaded wagons well towards the rear of the train, 66030 thunders through Oxford with 4O43, the 03.59 Wakefield Europort to Southampton Western Docks.
21 April 2018.

Still at Oxford, this is 66018 passing through with 4O21, the 09.15 Trafford Park to Southampton Western Docks. This loco has since received the latest DB red livery. 28 September 2015.

This is the view from the Osney Road footbridge at the southern end of Oxford station as 66128 rumbles along the through line with a well loaded 4O43, the 03.59 Wakefield Europort to Southampton Western Docks once again. Notice the new high intensity headlights now being fitted to many of the class. 15 March 2017.

Above: Sadly, this is another shot lost to overhead electrification as 66085 passes Pangbourne on the GWML with an unidentified engineers' train, probably heading for either Didcot or Hinksey Yard. 4 March 2009.

Left: The same loco 66085, now in DB red, is captured over the boundary fence at almost the same location as the previous image, this time heading east with 4O39, the 09.43 Morris Cowley to Southampton Eastern Docks car train. 5 October 2018.

Finding a path amongst the mass of electric units in this area, this is 66070 about to take the curve as it approaches Clapham Junction with 6Y91, the 10.40 Cliffe to Purley stone train. This loco has since received DB red. 26 February 2010.

Above: This time we see 66018 passing slowly through Paddock Wood with 6Y93, the 09.35 Purley to Cliffe empty stone train. This is another loco that is now in DB colours. 23 July 2010.

Right: This is another view of 6Y91, the 10.40 Cliffe to Purley stone train, this time hauled by 66147 and approaching South Croydon, another location that is usually very busy with electric units. 10 December 2008.

The first of two images at the same spot, same train, same loco! 66020 is powering towards Worting Junction, west of Basingstoke, with 4O39, the 09.43 Morris Cowley to Southampton Eastern Docks car train. 13 March 2017.

The only change is the livery of the loco as 66020 is seen again, approaching the camera almost exactly a year later. 21 March 2018.

66119 is seen entering the down loop line at Redbridge with a special train of military vehicles from the port at Marchwood. The train has travelled wrong line for about a mile or so after coming off the Fawley branch at Totton. 24 July 2007.

Nicely framed by the tunnel portal (shame about that signal gantry though), this is 66134 approaching Southampton Central with a Balfour Beatty cable laying train, heading west to an unknown destination. Even allowing for the fact that a telephoto lens was used, the state of the track is quite evident. It was actually renewed not long after this shot was taken. 4 November 2004.

This is 66241 passing beneath the Rockstone footbridge between Dawlish Warren and Dawlish with a short freight working from Exeter Riverside to St Blazey. I am not sure what the white marking is just to the left of the multiple-working socket, or if it has any significance? This loco is now working for DB Cargo France. 5 October 2003.

On a late summer's day, this is 66015 passing through Dawlish station with 6C12, the 10.57 Burngullow to Exeter Riverside sand train. 24 August 2019.

The famous Royal Albert Bridge is seen in the background as 66123 slowly comes across with 6C06, the 11.06 St Blazey to Tavistock Junction china clay empties. The signal box here had long been disused by this date. The loco is now at work in Europe for DB. 12 June 2004.

We now head back to the GWML at Didcot for a view of 66021 approaching with a merry-go-round coal train from Avonmouth destined for the power station in the background. Both the train service and power station are now long gone. 12 October 2012.

Now in DB red livery, 66021 passes through Eastleigh non-stop with 4O39, the 09.43 Morris Cowley to Southampton Eastern Docks car train. 29 March 2021.

Once again, before the overhead electrification transformed this location, this is 66075 passing Severn Tunnel Junction with 4E66, the 08.55 Margam to Redcar coal train. 6 January 2012.

66193 passes through Cardiff Central with an eastbound steel train, probably heading for Llanwern steelworks. This loco has since been sent to work for DB Cargo France. 7 September 2006.

Left: Absolutely immaculate in DB red, 66117 rumbles through Severn Tunnel Junction with 6V05, the 09.15 Round Oak to Margam steel train. 9 October 2018.

Below: Viewed from the St Philip's Causeway feeder road that crosses the line at North Somerset Junction (Bristol), this is 66090 after running round a DB cable laying train and pulling away from Bristol East sidings. The working was the 6Z60 13.36 Bristol Barton Hill to East Usk Yard. 20 January 2016.

This is another service that has unfortunately now ended, 66171 is passing Worting Junction with 6M66, the 09.32 Southampton Eastern Docks to Garston (Liverpool) car train. 27 April 2015.

Right: This is 66102 at the familiar location of Battledown Flyover, just east of Basingstoke, with 4O39, the 09.43 Morris Cowley to Southampton Eastern Docks. 5 April 2016.

Below: 66026 is seen at Freemantle, on the approach to Southampton Central, with 6Y27, the 10.12 Quidhampton to Eastleigh china clay train. This service ceased to run at the end of March 2009, and the loco itself was sent to work in France soon after that. 11 February 2004.

Looking in the opposite direction from the same vantage point as the previous image, this is 66146 soon after passing through Southampton Central with 6V62, the 13.34 Fawley to Tavistock Junction tank train, the loco having run round in Eastleigh Yard. Needless to say, this train no longer runs, and the loco is another one currently working abroad, this time in Poland for DB Cargo Polska. 2 September 2004.

Looking very smart in DB red, 66128 is approaching Shawford with 6M48, the 10.32 Southampton Eastern Docks to Halewood (Jaguar Cars). 10 November 2017.

Awaiting the signal at Basingstoke, this is 66078 with 4O43, the 03.59 Wakefield Europort to Southampton Western Docks intermodal service. 17 June 2021.

The paintwork is looking a bit tatty on the roof as 66061 is captured taking the Reading line soon after passing Basingstoke with 6M66, the 09.47 Southampton Western Docks to Garston car train. Since this picture was taken, the cutting sides here have once again become hopelessly overgrown. 15 June 2015.

With the bright yellow field to the left, it is undoubtedly spring time. Before its makeover in Maritime blue and naming as *Maritime Intermodal Two*, this is 66047 passing Mortimer on the Basingstoke to Reading line with 4Z69, the 09.32 Southampton Western Docks to Masborough. 28 April 2016.

At the same location as the previous image but a different perspective, this time we see 66116 with 6M48, the 10.32 Southampton Eastern Docks to Halewood. 12 May 2015.

Framed by the signals, 66029 is powering towards Shawford station in charge of 4M52, the 10.34 Southampton Eastern Docks to Castle Bromwich 'blue sausage' car train. This is another loco that has since been sent to work for DB Cargo France. 19 June 2003.

Slowly approaching the signal at Campbell Road at Eastleigh, this is 66239 with 6B44, the 12.07 Southampton Docks to Eastleigh Yard trip working. Inevitably, this is another Class 66 now working on the other side of the English Channel. 24 January 2005.

66050 *EWS Energy* is seen passing Basingstoke with 6M48, the 10.32 Southampton Eastern Docks to Halewood. Considering that EWS became DB Schenker in 2009 and later DB Cargo, it is somewhat surprising that this loco still carries its name. 12 January 2022.

An image now impossible to replicate due to the removal of the footbridge I was standing on, 66028 is coming out of the docks complex with 6B44, the 12.07 Southampton Docks to Eastleigh Yard trip working. This is another loco that was sent to work in Europe for DB Cargo France, but during 2021 it was returned to Toton depot to be converted back to UK specification. 14 April 2004.

Passing over the recently relaid pointwork at Eastleigh, this is 66228 heading south with 7O48, the Whatley to Hamworthy stone train. This loco is also currently working in France. 24 January 2005.

The first of a few images of the sand workings to Wool in Dorset. Curving round to pass through Southampton Central, 66062 leads 6M42, the 14.00 Wool to Neasden. EWS locos initially worked this train in the early 2000s, but it was taken over by Freightliner during 2006, and has now ceased to run altogether. This loco is also currently in France. 18 February 2004.

After splitting the train, this is 66064 having just departed Eastleigh Yard with the first portion of the Neasden to Wool sand train. Another of the class currently working for DB Cargo France. 20 August 2003.

This time 66085 is captured departing Dorchester South after the loco had run round in the station, the train then commencing its trip back to Wool so as to access the siding adjacent to the up side platform at Wool station. This loco has since been painted in DB red. 24 March 2004.

A few years later, the working was revised to bring the whole train to Dorchester South, then part of the train was shunted into the one remaining siding located here and split into two parts. This is the first portion, just east of Moreton, headed by 66180. On arrival at Wool, the loco would then go back light engine to Dorchester to collect the remaining wagons for loading, and when completed the whole train would depart for Neasden. This loco is currently working in Poland. 10 April 2008.

Remaining in Dorset, this is an unusual shot of 66062 taking the reverse curves on the approach to Hamworthy with 6W53, the 08.45 Eastleigh Yard to Furzebrook LPG train. This train is long since consigned to history, and the loco is currently working in France. 22 April 2005.

Still at Hamworthy on the same day, this is 66201 in the former down loop line about to depart down the short freight-only branch to Hamworthy Quay with an empty train to be loaded with scrap metal for Cardiff Tidal. The semaphore signal is not actually connected to anything, despite appearances. 22 April 2005.

Later in the morning, at Hamworthy Quay, 66201 is seen again while some of its wagons are being loaded. Unfortunately, at the time of writing, there have not been any trains down this branch for some years now. 22 April 2005.

This time we are at the pre-rebuilt Reading station as 66118 passes through with 6V18, the 12.35 Hither Green to Whatley empty stone train. The loco was one of the early ones to receive DB red livery, and although the train still runs today, it is now Freightliner-hauled. 30 June 2011.

Brand new 66248 is seen at Newport Godfrey Road stabling point. This loco was one of the final batch of EWS machines to be delivered and was offloaded from the ship at Newport Docks on 21 June 2000 and is seen here just three days later. It has since been sent to work for DB Cargo Polska. 24 June 2000.

Seen from the Freemantle footbridge just to the west of Southampton Central, 66138 approaches with 6B62, the 09.13 Fawley to Eastleigh Yard oil train, which no longer runs. This particular loco has been stored at Toton depot since October 2018. 11 February 2004.

From the same location but 14 years later, 66136 is approaching with the short-lived overnight 6O11, the 10.00 Dowlow Briggs Sidings to Southampton Up Yard stone train. Just over a year earlier, the loco had worked from Dollands Moor with the first through train from Yiwu, China, to the UK, which had travelled via the Channel Tunnel, hence the adornments on the loco. 1 February 2018.

A series of views on the GWML now, which of course have mostly become impossible since electrification. Heading west on the approach to Twyford, 66055 has charge of 6B35, the 10.46 Hayes and Harlington to Moreton on Lugg empty stone train. Note the additional headlight fitted to the front of this loco, which is intended to assist with coupling when the loco is used as a Lickey Incline banking engine, one of three of the class so fitted. It is also now in DB red livery and carrying the name *Alain Thauvette*. 13 November 2013.

Further west, we see 66230 passing through Tilehurst with 6M48, the 10.32 Southampton Eastern Docks to Halewood. This loco was involved in a serious altercation with a staff transport buggy at Dollands Moor during 2018, and, as a result, one of the cabs was totally burnt out. It is now in store at Toton and unlikely to work again. 13 March 2014.

With autumn colours in evidence all around, 66046 passes Lower Basildon with 6V27, the 13.30 Eastleigh to Hinksey Yard engineers' train. This loco was sold by DB in 2017 and is now transformed into 66782 working for GBRf. The train itself still runs today but now with Colas Rail traction. 28 October 2009.

A little further west and we see 66237 passing through the local lines at Didcot Parkway with 6B35, the 10.46 Hayes and Harlington to Moreton on Lugg empty stone train. This loco currently earns a living with DB Cargo Polska. 3 March 2010.

One of the very first locos to be repainted in DB red, 66097 exits the power station at Didcot with a few crippled wagons. This was believed to be one of the last rail moves from the facility. 30 June 2011.

Further west, we arrive at Swindon, where 66178 is approaching with one of the regular coal trains that ran to and from Didcot Power Station to Avonmouth, now long consigned to history. This loco is also now in Poland. 23 April 2009.

Just north of Didcot on the line to Oxford, this view was taken from the footbridge at Didcot North Junction as a very smart 66130 takes the station line with 4O39, the 09.43 Morris Cowley to Southampton Eastern Docks car train, which usually lays over in Didcot Yard for a couple of hours or so. 5 April 2018.

From the next bridge up, which can be seen in the previous picture, this is 66182 with the same car train coming around the long sweeping curve. 17 November 2016.

Geoff Spencer

Moving a little further north, we see DB red 66066 *Geoff Spencer* passing through the quiet station at Radley, just south of Oxford, with Colas Rail-operated 6M50, the 07.59 Westbury to Bescot engineers' train. The loco was believed to be hired-in by Colas due to no Class 66/8 or Class 70 being available that morning at Westbury. 10 September 2019.

Just west of Southampton Central is Millbrook station, where we now see a series of shots. 66225 passes through with 7O48, the Whatley to Hamworthy stone train. This loco is currently working in France. In 2020, the portion of footbridge from which this view was taken was removed, making this shot now impossible. 30 November 2004.

Heading in the opposite direction is 66216 with 6B62, the 09.13 Fawley to Eastleigh Yard oil train. This is another loco currently working for DB Cargo France, and the train has now ceased to run. 14 July 2004.

Another of the early DB red repaints was 66101, seen drifting through with the very lightly loaded 6V41, the 14.45 Eastleigh Yard to Westbury engineers' train. This service still runs today but is now worked by GBRf traction. 16 August 2011.

The last view at Millbrook as 66222 approaches with an interesting load consisting of a couple of Kirow cranes and support wagons forming 6O41, the 10.14 Westbury to Eastleigh Yard. This working has since been taken over by GBRf, and this loco is another one currently in Europe. 17 December 2003.

Left: This is a very clean 66034 at Heywood village, just north of Westbury, with the 6M20 09.23 Whatley Quarry to Churchyard Sidings. The usual route for this train would be more direct via the Berks and Hants line through Newbury, but, at this time, there was a planned closure in that area for electrification work. This train has since gone over to Freightliner haulage. 10 July 2018.

Below: In the lovely surroundings of the Avon Valley between Westbury & Bath, this is 66207 with 6C83, the 13.40 Avonmouth Bennets Siding to Westbury. 12 April 2014.

Millbrook Freightliner terminal is in the background as 66232 heads west towards Redbridge with an unidentified train loaded with ballast. Inevitably, this is another Class 66 now abroad in France. 13 June 2014.

Looking in the opposite direction from this now closed footbridge, 66097 passes by with 6V38, the 11.00 Marchwood to Eastleigh Ministry of Defence (MoD) train. Most of the occasional traffic to and from the military port at Marchwood is now in the hands of GBRf. 1 May 2013.

RAILWAY HERITAGE COMMITTEE

Approaching Lambert's Bridge just west of Westbury is 66200 *Railway Heritage Committee* with 6M20, the 09.23 Whatley Quarry to Churchyard Sidings stone train. This train now operates under the Freightliner banner. This loco has since been de-named. 7 August 2015.

On a bright winter afternoon in Somerset, 66192 is captured at Wyke Champflower, just north of Castle Cary, with 6C97, the 08.20 Pilning to Westbury, which had gone to Fairwater Yard (Taunton) so the loco could run round. 7 January 2018.

From a footbridge across the line that was a fine vantage point near Tilehurst, but now lost to electrification, we see 66124 approaching with 4O39, the 09.43 Morris Cowley to Southampton Eastern Docks car train. 13 March 2014.

Now in DB red, 66124 is approaching Westbury off the Trowbridge line with 6B35, the 09.50 Wembley Yard to Whatley Quarry, yet another short-term flow that has now ceased. 9 February 2018.

Ever since the heritage Swanage Railway was reconnected to the national network back in the early 2000s, various sporadic infrastructure trains have operated over the branch. Having run light engine from Eastleigh earlier in the day, this is 66213 just about to pass under the A351 at Norden with the 6Z41 Swanage to Eastleigh Yard with a rake of ballast wagons. These had been taken down a couple of months beforehand for the use of the Swanage Railway. 26 February 2008.

The same train with 66213 is now seen further up the branch towards Wareham and about to pass under a minor road bridge about a mile south of Worgret Junction. The overgrown mess that you see here was subsequently totally cleared a few years later when the Swanage Railway took over this section and is now transformed completely. The loco itself is currently at work in Europe. 26 February 2008.

Resourceful

One of the more recent DB repaints, 66035 *Resourceful* (a name once carried by 47594, which also carried the number 47035 as its first TOPS identity) is approaching Romsey with 6O41, the 10.14 Westbury to Eastleigh. The loco was hired in by GBRf on this particular day as none of its own traction was available at Westbury. 8 January 2019.

The DB livery certainly stands out, especially when clean. 66149 with a rake of similar-coloured wagons rounds the tight curve onto the Romsey line at Redbridge Junction with 6V41, the 14.45 Eastleigh Yard to Westbury. This was a far better view before the horrible fence was erected many years ago! 9 March 2017.

Viewed from over a hedgerow at Kimbridge, west of Romsey, this is 66113 with the same train as the last image; the 6V41 14.45 Eastleigh–Westbury. The loco has since been transformed by an application of DB red and the addition of vinyls to acknowledge the work done by key workers during the 2020/21 coronavirus pandemic. Many years ago, this location was near to a junction for the so-called 'Sprat & Winkle Line', which used to run from Redbridge to Andover and closed back in 1967. 20 March 2009.

A rather battered-looking 66089 approaches Southampton Airport Parkway with 4O43, the 03.59 Wakefield Europort to Southampton Western Docks. The airport itself is out of view to the right of the picture. 16 May 2013.

Another view of 6V41, the 14.45 Eastleigh Yard to Westbury, before it changed to GBRf traction, as 66053 passes St Denys heading south with a good load. 9 September 2010.

On the approach to Basingstoke station, this is 66246 heading north with a short consist, including a Balfour Beatty crane on the rear, forming 6V27, the 13.30 Eastleigh to Hinksey. This is now a Colas Rail service, and the loco is currently working in France. 27 September 2004.

A conveniently situated multi-storey car park provides an unusual view of the final loco of the EWS Class 66 fleet. This is 66250 approaching Basingstoke with 4M52, the 10.34 Southampton Eastern Docks to Castle Bromwich car train. In late 2017, this was one of the locos sold by DB to GBRf and is now something of a celebrity, working under the guise of 66789 in BR large logo blue livery and named *British Rail 1948-1997*. 30 June 2015.

66224 nears Micheldever with 6M44, the 13.30 Eastleigh Yard to Wembley 'Enterprise' service, which is unfortunately now discontinued. It is a shame that this location has been made more difficult by the addition of another few rows of bricks on the parapets to raise the height, thwarting any attempt to get the camera in position, unless of course you happen to carry a step ladder or be about 8ft tall! The loco is currently at work in Europe. 15 April 2003.

This is 66043 departing Eastleigh with 4O43, the 03.59 Wakefield Europort to Southampton Western Docks. This loco was put into storage in May 2017 and has not worked since. 2 October 2015.

The 4O43 03.59 Wakefield Europort to Southampton Western Docks is seen again, this time passing through Southampton Central with 66243 in charge. The loco is another currently working for DB Cargo in France. 11 July 2006.

Absolutely sparkling in ex-works DB red, 66206 approaches Southampton Central in the opposite direction from the previous image with 4M71, the 09.47 Southampton Western Docks to Birch Coppice intermodal service. 8 May 2017.

About to pass a curious-looking colour light signal, 66085 nears Wilton Junction, a couple of miles west of Salisbury, with 6X41, the 10.14 Westbury to Eastleigh. Although it is impossible to tell from this view, near to where the yellow tilted-deck point-carrying wagons are in the train was located Wilton North GWR station, which was closed as long ago as 1955. Very few images exist of it. 3 April 2015.

Heading west at Wilton Junction from the same bridge in the previous shot, this is 66086 with a diverted 6M48, the 10.34 Southampton Eastern Docks to Halewood. The lines to the right are the former Southern Railway West of England route to Exeter via Yeovil. 3 April 2015.

Above: Slowly proceeding along the down loop at Banbury, this is 66037 with 4O21, the 09.15 Trafford Park Euro Terminal to Southampton Western Docks intermodal. 19 December 2014.

Left: This time we see 66050 *EWS Energy* passing through the South London suburbs near Chiswick with 6Y42, the 09.00 Eastleigh Yard to Hoo Junction engineers' train. This service has since changed to GBRf haulage. 30 April 2010.

Taken from a public foot crossing just west of Salisbury, this is 66210 approaching with 6Y27, the 10.28 Quidhampton to Eastleigh calcium carbonate slurry tanks. This train no longer runs, the loco is working in France and the photographers on the bridge in the distance were waiting for a 'Black 5' steam-hauled charter. 12 April 2006.

The low angle creates a powerful perspective of 66038 as it passes through Eastleigh station with 7O48, the Whatley Quarry to Hamworthy stone train. Once again, this loco currently resides in France. 24 March 2003.

Right: Although it is early springtime in the Avon Valley, there is not a lot of greenery to be seen as 66096 approaches Avoncliff Halt with 6C83, the 13.40 Avonmouth Bennets Siding to Westbury service. The River Avon is prominent in the foreground. 30 March 2012.

Below: On a fine, frosty winter morning, we see 66114 at Norton Bavant, just east of Warminster, with 6O41, the 10.14 Westbury to Eastleigh engineers' train. This loco was another early recipient of DB red livery, and the train it is hauling is now operated by GBRf. 20 January 2011.

This is 66218 passing through Newport with a westbound steel train, probably bound for Llanwern. This view is rather different nowadays due to the overhead electrification. The loco now operates in Europe. 2 July 2003.

Seemingly rising up out of a large hole in the ground, this is 66170 coming up the 1 in 80 gradient from the St Denys direction across the River Itchen bridge and approaching Bitterne with 6Y32, the 08.13 Fawley to Holybourne tanks. 23 December 2015.

Looking very bright in the sunshine is 66185 *DP World London Gateway* as it passes through Winchfield station with 7O12, the 04.26 Merehead Quarry to Woking stone train. This service has now switched to Freightliner haulage. 23 September 2016.

Just over a week earlier, the same Woking-bound stone train as seen in the previous image was hauled by 66061 and is captured a little further east along the South Western Main Line near Fleet. 14 September 2016.

Semaphore signals aplenty here as the driver of 66223 collects the token from the signaller at Marchwood as he proceeds a little further down the single line to pick up the daily train from the MoD complex. Unfortunately, this is no longer a runner, and the loco is in France. 4 August 2003.

Somewhere underneath this unbelievable grime is 66199! The loco is seen taking the depot line at Eastleigh heading for a long overdue wash and brush up. It had of course just finished a long spell on Railhead Treatment Train duties. 25 November 2011.

Alain Thauvette

In contrast to the previous image, a nice clean 66055 *Alain Thauvette*, one of the more recent namings, passes Worting Junction, west of Basingstoke, with the 4M71 09.47 Southampton Western Docks to Birch Coppice. The tail end of a southbound container train can be seen heading into the distance. This is one of three locos used for banking duties on the Lickey Incline and is fitted with a light on the front end to aid coupling in the dark. 24 September 2019.

A fine autumn afternoon sees 66127 passing Salisbury with 6V41, the 14.45 Eastleigh Yard to Westbury engineers' train. 6 November 2017.

The well-known view next to Westbury station sees 66245 engaged in a spot of shunting. Yes, you have guessed it, this is another loco currently working in France for DB Cargo. 28 February 2005.

Immaculate 66115 is seen at Lambert's Bridge, just west of Westbury, with 6M20, the 10.37 Whatley Quarry to Churchyard Sidings (St Pancras) stone train. This service is now in the hands of Freightliner, as are many workings in this area at present. 26 April 2018.

This is 66248 slowly passing Eastleigh with 6V38, the 11.40 Marchwood to Didcot MoD train, yet another service that ceased some years ago and another loco working at the present time in Poland. 31 July 2008.

Like most former vantage points along the GWML this location has unfortunately been lost to electrification. 66156 comes around the curves near Moulsford in the Thames Valley with an unidentified southbound intermodal heading for Southampton Western Docks. 2 September 2011.

Even after almost 24 years, 66002 still looks pretty smart as it departs Eastleigh with a set of newly-refurbished car carrying wagons heading for Southampton Eastern Docks. Like 66001, this loco does not feature an AAR auto-coupling due to differences in the construction of its frame. 28 January 2022.

Around a mile or so west of Southampton Central, 66231 is captured passing Millbrook station with 6V41, the 14.45 Eastleigh Yard to Westbury engineers' train. This loco is currently in France. 16 August 2005.

Amazing to think that the first of the class in DB red livery was painted as long ago as 2009. This is the first of a couple of shots of this loco. 66152 *Derek Holmes Railway Operator* (it was named during 2010) is seen approaching Southampton Central with 6B44, the 12.07 Southampton Western Docks to Eastleigh trip working. 13 May 2015.

This next image sees the loco awaiting to proceed at the signal at Campbell Road, Eastleigh, with 4M71, the 09.47 Southampton Western Docks to Birch Coppice intermodal. 5 July 2021.

The seven DB locos finished in the Maritime Transport blue customer livery during the late 2010s are primarily intended for intermodal trains, but they have inevitably found their way onto other DB services. This is ex-works 66162 *Maritime Intermodal Five* approaching Eastleigh with 6M48, the 10.32 Southampton Eastern Docks to Halewood. 2 October 2019.

This is the 'blue sausage' cartics again, this time with 66242 heading north through St Denys with 4M52, the 10.34 Southampton Eastern Docks to Castle Bromwich. 13 May 2004.

Also heading north through St Denys is 66200 with 6B44, the 12.07 Southampton Western Docks to Eastleigh Yard trip working. By this date, the loco had already lost its *Railway Heritage Committee* nameplates. 10 May 2016.

Hardly worth the effort this one! 66238 exits Southampton Tunnel with the very sparsely loaded 6B45, the 09.10 Eastleigh Yard to MoD Marchwood trip. This train no longer runs, and the loco was sold to GBRf in 2017, now carrying the identity of 66788. 15 August 2007.

James Nightall G.C.

Above: A location now lost to undergrowth, this is 66079 *James Nightall GC* heading south through Shawford with a totally empty 4O43, the 03.59 Wakefield to Southampton Western Docks. 24 March 2014.

Right: It is always nice to see immaculate rolling stock, especially when it is a freight train! Newly repainted 66165 is seen in the unloading area at Bevois Park (now known as Southampton Up Yard) with the short-term overnight 6O11, the 10.00 Dowlow Briggs Sidings to Southampton Up Yard stone train. 15 February 2018.

Sometimes nicknamed the 'pongliner' (you would understand that when it passes close by), this is 6C03, the 09.33 Northolt Sidings to Sita, Severnside, containerised refuse service, heading through Reading with 66097 at the helm. 5 May 2021.

Chapter 2

Charters and Specials

Perhaps inevitably, many of the Class 66/0 fleet have also been used on charter trains, multiple unit drags and other stock moves and special workings during their time in service, with some even making it onto heritage lines.

Left: The unmistakeable location of the famous sea wall section at Dawlish sees 66107 hauling a rake of Great Western HST stock as 5Z43, the 22.22 Kilmarnock to Laira. This was one of the last occasions a DB loco worked these moves before Rail Operations Group took over. Of course, now that front line HSTs have ceased with GWR, these moves no longer take place. The loco itself is now in DB red livery. 28 August 2015.

Below: Two views of 66024 top and tailing 66209 as they haul brand new 444004 south from Eastleigh to Bournemouth depot. This image shows the ensemble as it leaves the East Yard. Quite often, these moves happened during darkness and at awkward times, so were quite tricky to photograph. 66209 is now working in France. 23 December 2003.

Back then, the new 'Desiro' units were brought through the Channel Tunnel as far as Eastleigh Yard, then tripped to either Northam or Bournemouth depots. 66209 brings up the rear as the ensemble seen in the previous image passes through Eastleigh station and heads south. 23 December 2003.

Right: This is 66003 with one of the later deliveries heading south through St Denys hauling brand new 444039 from Eastleigh Yard to Bournemouth with another unidentified member of the class on the rear. 27 January 2005.

Below: This time we see 66011 heading though Southampton Central hauling a brand-new Class 377 unit for temporary storage at MoD Marchwood on the Fawley branch. A number of these units were stored due to the delays they encountered when entering traffic during the mid-2000s. 9 January 2004.

Above: Crossing the Grosvenor Bridge over the River Thames at Chelsea, 66144 is hauling 442404 as the 5Z67 Brighton Lovers Walk to Wolverton. At this time, various Class 442 units were heading to/from Wolverton for attention when they were in service with Southern/Gatwick Express. 17 September 2010.

Left: Amongst all the modern paraphernalia associated with electrification, this is the DB red-liveried pair of 66084 and 66020 passing the original station buildings at Tilehurst on the GWML with no less than 16 coaches in tow, this forming the 5Z45 09.40 Eastleigh Works to Burton Wetmore Sidings stock move. 7 January 2022.

The first of three images depicting the historic first passenger train from London to Swanage since the late 1960s. Not long after its repaint into DB red livery, this is 66152 at East Holme, about a mile or so south of Worgret Junction on the newly reopened section of the Swanage Branch, with 1Z98, the 08.45 London Victoria to Swanage 'Purbeck Pioneer' charter. 1 April 2009.

Above: The crowds were out at Swanage station for the arrival of the train as 66152 draws to a halt at the heritage line's terminus. 1 April 2009.

Right: It was a magnificent day for this event, with the sun shining all day. The return 1Z91, the 16.05 Swanage to London Waterloo, was worked by EWS-liveried 66142 (since painted in Maritime blue). The train is seen from the superb vantage point of the famous ruined castle as it passes slowly through Corfe Castle station, heading back up the branch towards the main line at Worgret Junction. 1 April 2009.

Back to just after the turn of the 21st century now as we see the 1Z91 08.42 Finsbury Park to Bristol Temple Meads 'Avon Lady', one of the first charters of the new millennium, arriving at Bristol Temple Meads behind a comparatively new 66030. 8 January 2000.

A little later in the same year, 66059 and 33103 are seen at Poole on the rear of 1Z36, the 04.46 Crewe to Poole via Hamworthy 'The Dorset Mariner' charter. This whole day was a bit of a mess by all accounts, as the train originally started out double-headed by 33109+33103, but 33109 developed a problem en route and was removed at Swindon, with this and various other problems all leading to some late running and missed itineraries. 15 April 2000.

Just under a year later, the train was re-run (I believe free of charge to all who were on the train in the previous image) due to all these problems. This is 66222 approaching Hamworthy Junction with 1Z92, the 06.05 Crewe to Southampton via Hamworthy Quay and Furzebrook 'Dorset Mariner 2' charter. This loco has since found work in Europe with DB Cargo. 24 March 2001.

The train was top and tailed throughout, and on the other end was 66194, seen at Sterte on the approach to Poole with the return from both of the Dorset freight branches. 24 March 2001.

Arriving at the Dorset coastal resort destination for this charter, this is 66063 with 1Z27, the 09.36 Bristol Temple Meads to Weymouth 'Dorset Coast Express'. On the other end of the train is ex GWR 'King' 6024 *King Edward 1* on one of its rare visits to this location. In subsequent years, this charter has become quite popular and has run a few times most summers. 1 August 2008.

Despite appearances, this is not a heritage line! 66101 clatters along the jointed track and bullhead rails near Thornford with the Weymouth to Yeovil Junction leg of a 'Cathedrals Express' charter that started earlier in the day at London Victoria, travelling to Weymouth via Bournemouth with A1 60163 *Tornado*. The steam loco was reattached at Yeovil Junction after servicing and took the train via Gillingham back to London. 17 August 2011.

This time we see 66088 on the rear of 1Z16, the 09.43 London Victoria to Fawley 'The Swaythling Bands' charter. 66023 was on the front at this point as the train passes Millbrook. 8 December 2015.

66041 approaches Fairwood Junction, soon after passing through Westbury, with the first leg of a UK Railtours' operated three-day tour from London to Devon and Cornwall, named 'The West Countryman'. This loco has since received DB red livery. 25 September 2009.

Also near Westbury, but this time approaching from the easterly direction, this is 66105 with 1Z23, the 07.22 London Paddington to Bristol Temple Meads via Westbury Yard 'Only Freight Track and Horses'. The train was top and tailed with Freightliner's 66514 and covered a variety of freight yards and lines around the Bristol area. 11 September 2021.

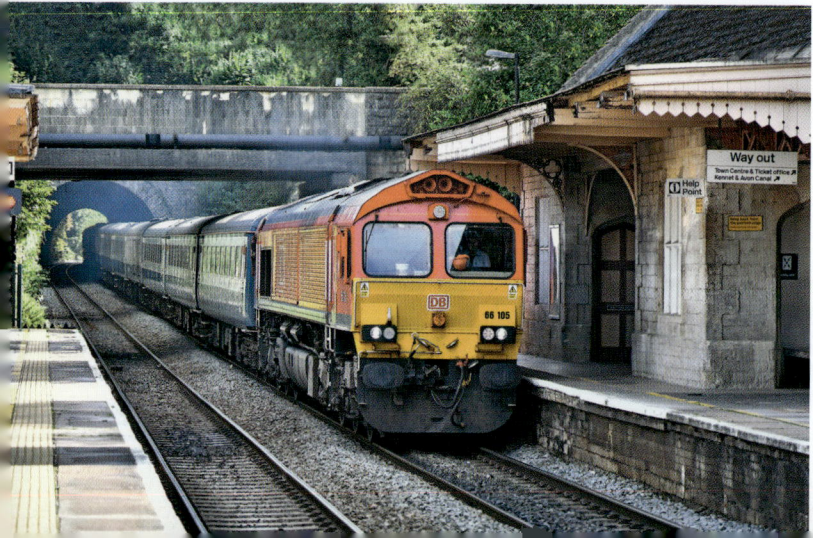

The train seen in the previous image is captured again as it heads through the fine Brunel-designed Bradford on Avon station heading for Bristol. 11 September 2021.

It is not often one of the class can be seen on the Belmond British Pullman, but this was the case here as 66142 pulls away from the brief stop at Westbury with 1V80, the 09.47 London Victoria to Bristol Temple Meads. This loco is now in blue and named *Maritime Intermodal Three*. 30 August 2006.

Four years on, and another instance occurred as we see 66250 (the future 66789) heading west through Paddock Wood with 1Y46, the 10.48 London Victoria to Folkestone West British Pullman charter. 25 March 2010.

66023 top and tails 66088 as they approach Farnborough with 5Z01, the 07.51 Eastleigh depot to London Victoria empty stock move. The pair later worked a charter to Ashford. 9 December 2015.

In a heavy downpour, 66230 passes Basingstoke with 5Z47, the 12.49 Eastleigh Works to Crewe Holding Sidings, with a short rake of empty stock. The unfortunate fate of this loco was detailed earlier in this volume. 29 March 2018.

In far better weather, 66007 is seen at the same spot with a similar working, the 5Z52 09.57 Eastleigh Works to Tyseley Steam Trust, with another short rake of empty coaches. 3 April 2019.

Another rake of empty stock, this is 5Z64, the 11.03 Eastleigh Works to Tyseley Steam Trust, this time a little further west of Basingstoke and hauled by an immaculate 66100 *Armistice 100 1918-2018*. 4 September 2019.

This is 66086 departing Eastleigh East Yard with an unidentified working of Mk.2 coaches that I believe were heading either to Southampton Docks for export, or to MoD Marchwood for storage. 17 May 2007.

With its unique white cab roofs, 66177 passes Eastleigh with Royal coach 2916 running as 5Z50 from Wolverton to Eastleigh Works, the Mk.3 going for a bogie overhaul. The application of the white paint was an experiment to help with cab temperatures by reflecting sunlight, but it did not progress further. 29 December 2021.

A pretty unusual working as 66126 passes Sevington, just west of Ashford, with the 7Z80 Dollands Moor to Warrington Arpley, complete with Freightliner's 70007 in the middle of the consist. The Class 70 was brand new and had been on display in Berlin at Innotrans 2010. It was the only one of the class to be delivered to the UK via the Channel Tunnel. Interestingly, 66126 has since gone on long-term hire to Direct Rail Services (DRS) and is now in the company's dark blue livery. 8 October 2010.

Another one-off working at Salisbury as 66138 has ex Southern Railway 'Lord Nelson' 850 *Lord Nelson* in tow behind a few barrier wagons heading west from Eastleigh Works to the West Somerset Railway. The steam loco had just undergone a full restoration and was going for testing and running in at the preserved line before venturing out onto the main line. The Class 66 has been stored at Toton since October 2018, and *Lord Nelson* now resides on the Mid Hants Railway. 16 August 2006.

The final couple of images in this section show EWS saloons that have since been taken out of use. This first image illustrates 66115 heading west at Cockwood Harbour, near Starcross, hauling two examples, DM45020 and DB999509. They were bound for the naval dockyard at Devonport, just west of Plymouth, where they were used as escort coaches for the nuclear flask trains that originated there. This loco now carries DB red. 15 August 2002.

A little earlier the same month, 66202 is captured approaching Plymouth with saloon DM45020 heading east and bound for an unknown destination. The loco is now working in France. 1 August 2002.

Chapter 3

Pairs, Triples and More!

For me personally, I always find it fascinating to see more than one loco at the front of a train, regardless of the type. In this day and age though, it is more common than one might think. Here are just a few that I have observed over the last 20 years or so. Most of these instances though are due to the need for an extra loco being required elsewhere, rather than any extra horsepower.

Various detail differences can be seen as the first and last locos of the EWS order are seen side by side, 66001 and 66250 being on display at the Old Oak Common open day. The final loco 66250 carried a small dedication below the EWS logo on the cabsides stating 'In Memory of Robert K. Romak', who was the Class 66 Project Engineer in London, Ontario, who died of cancer during the assembly of 66250. 1 August 2000.

Some years prior to this particular train changing to GBRf traction, 66007 and 60073 (formerly *Cairn Gorm*) are seen approaching Salisbury with 6O41, the 10.14 Westbury to Eastleigh. While the Class 66 is still in front line service, the Class 60 has long since been withdrawn. 26 November 2009.

There was a period around the late 2000s when DB was faced with a bit of a dilemma, as its Class 60 locos were starting to become a tad failure prone with only a few available for service, but DB found it still required their superior haulage power on some of its heavier trains. For this reason, pairs of Class 66s were briefly trialled as replacements, but this practice never seemed to be very successful and most of these heavy trains have reverted back to haulage by refurbished Class 60s. This is 66007 and 66117 approaching Cam & Dursley with 6B13, the 07.15 Robeston to Westerleigh. 5 March 2010.

A very cold morning sees 66047 and 66053 approaching Tilehurst with 6B33, the 13.35 Theale to Robeston tanks. 66047 has recently been given the Maritime blue livery and named *Maritime Intermodal Two*. 22 December 2009.

This is 6B13, the 07.15 Robeston to Westerleigh seen again, this time soon after exiting the lengthy tunnel at Wickwar, between Gloucester and Bristol, this time in the hands of 66197 and 66167. 8 April 2010.

Above: Many double-headed trains are run simply to avoid an extra light engine move, such is the case here. This is 66210 and 66234 approaching Eastleigh with 6O41, the 10.14 Westbury to Eastleigh infrastructure service. Both of these locos are currently working in Europe. 20 August 2003.

Right: 66235 and 60049 are seen in platform 2 at Eastleigh waiting to proceed onto the East Yard, having just come from the depot. 66235 is now working in Europe, while the Class 60 has been withdrawn from service. 21 December 2003.

6O41, the 10.14 Westbury to Eastleigh, is seen again, this time at Little Langford in the Wylye Valley, between Warminster and Salisbury, headed by 66125 and 66083. 18 July 2017.

An unusual pairing at Eastleigh as 66140 has 47810 and a few wagons attached. The loco later hauled the Class 47 north, eventually to Crewe as it had been acquired by Locomotive Services. It has since been restored to original BR two-tone green livery and regularly works main line charters. 18 April 2018.

Occasionally, some of the locos operated in France and neighbouring countries are tripped back via the Channel Tunnel, eventually destined for Toton for heavy repairs. This was the case here, as 66156 is seen hauling Euro-spec 66010 through Didcot Parkway heading north. More recently, 66010 is one of several examples that have, after a few modifications, returned to work in the UK in 2022. 3 September 2010.

Coming up the short, sharp gradient at Oakley, where the up South Western Bournemouth and Weymouth line rises to cross the line to Salisbury and Exeter at Battledown Flyover, this is 66162 and 66170 with 6M44, the 13.31 Eastleigh Yard to Wembley 'Enterprise' service. 66162 is another example now in blue livery and carrying the name *Maritime Intermodal Five*. 13 September 2012.

With both locos still quite new, 66199 and 67009 are stabled in the bay siding at Newton Abbot. At this time, celebrations were taking place for the Newton Abbot Festival of Transport over the whole weekend. 13 May 2000.

66231 and 37402 *Bont Y Bermo* are seen at Westbury during the process of moving the Class 37 from Eastleigh up to Crewe. I believe it may have first been moved to Cardiff Canton, and from there to Crewe at some point. 66231 is now working for DB Cargo France, and the Class 37 is still in occasional use with DRS. 4 February 2004.

Although taken recently, this image shows how quickly things can change on today's railways. 66058 in the foreground was at Eastleigh Works to undergo a transformation into 66783 *The Flying Dustman* in bright orange Biffa livery after purchase by GBRf, while behind is 66230, which has suffered a very different fate as described earlier in this volume. 19 January 2018.

Another loco balancing move, this time 66150 and 59103 are captured approaching Twyford with 7C77, the 12.41 Acton to Merehead Quarry. Overhead electrification has now dashed this view for good. The Class 66 is now in DB red livery and its forerunner owned by Freightliner. 17 September 2014.

On a lovely summer's day, this is 66140 and 66120 approaching the site of the long-closed Charlton Mackrell station, west of Castle Cary in Somerset, hauling MPV DR98907+DR98957 as 3Z15, the 12.20 Didcot Yard to St Blazey. 13 June 2021.

A triple this time as we see 66006, 67023 and 67027 with 6O15, the 16.57 Mossend to Eastleigh Yard, running 140 minutes late on the approach to Shawford, not far from its destination. This is another train that no longer runs. Interestingly, these two Class 67s later went on to work with Colas Rail, and in 2022 for GBRf. 10 December 2010.

It is not often that one can see DB and Freightliner locos in the same train. This was the case here, however, as 66040, 66524 and 66560 approach Eastleigh with 6O41, the 10.14 Westbury to Eastleigh. The two Freightliner locos were dead in train. 18 November 2016.

A Class 37 sandwich! 66008, 37422 and 66122 make a fine sight on the approach to Shawford, soon after setting off with 6M44, the 13.31 Eastleigh Yard to Wembley 'Enterprise' service. Although the Class 37 is still just about in service today with DRS, the Class 66s have had rather different fates. 66008 has been sold on by DB and has now become 66780 *The Cemex Express* working for GBRf, and 66122 is now in DRS dark blue livery and on long-term hire to that company. Once again, this is another train that has ceased running, the last one being in 2010. 13 June 2008.

66066 leads 66097 and 59205 up the steep grade at Dilton Marsh, soon after departing with 6O41, the 10.14 Westbury to Eastleigh Yard. Although the driver could probably have made good use of all this potential horsepower, it was just the front loco powering. The leading '66' is now in DB red livery and named *Geoff Spencer*. 30 March 2012.

This is 6M44, the 13.31 Eastleigh Yard to Wembley 'Enterprise', seen approaching Basingstoke with 66067, 66050 and 67010 up front. The Class 67 was a particularly unusual visitor to the area, being a dedicated Caledonian Sleeper loco at the time. 24 February 2016.

A nice uniform triple this time, as 66135, 66043 and 66108 pass Worting Junction, west of Basingstoke, with 6Y42, the 09.02 Eastleigh Yard to Hoo Junction, a service now in the care of GBRf. All change here as well loco-wise, as 66135 is now in DB red, 66043 has been stored for almost five years and 66108 is in DRS dark blue livery and on hire. 13 September 2012.

Not exactly a triple header but three together nonetheless! Back when locos literally formed a queue to exit Eastleigh depot to work various trains, this is another palindromic loco 66166, behind 66152 and 66064 on the depot exit road. Of these locos, 66166 is currently working in Poland, 66152 was the first of the class to receive DB red livery in 2009, and 66064 is currently working in Europe for DB Cargo France. 20 August 2003.

Nicely parked at the former Godfrey Road stabling point at Newport, 66185, 66204 and 66166 make an interesting image. Only 66185 is still working in the UK at the time of writing, now in DB red livery and named *DP World London Gateway*. 25 July 2001.

Straight out of the box this time! Three brand new locos, 66241, 66242 and 66248, are also seen at the Godfrey Road stabling point, having literally just come from the quayside after delivery from the USA. None of these locos are currently working in the UK, with 66241 and 66242 being employed with DB Cargo France and 66248 with DB Cargo Polska. 24 June 2000.

A foursome this time, unfortunately not the best quality image though on this very dark day, but it is one that shows the final working of 66238, 66058, 66015 and 66046 before all were transformed into GBRf locos after sale by DB. 66238 is now 66788, 66058 became 66783, 66016 emerged as 66781, and 66046 morphed into 66782. The convoy is passing Winchfield as 0O65, the 09.27 Peterborough to Eastleigh Works. 19 December 2017.

We now see a quintuplet as 66087, 66131, 66127, 66068 and 66154 approach Freshford in the Avon Valley, between Bath and Bradford on Avon, with the Saturdays-only 0O12 10.53 Margam to Eastleigh convoy. This working is well known for sometimes being as many as ten locos. Of this group, 66131 is now in DB red but the rest are unchanged. 20 October 2012.

A quintuplet on its own is one thing, but when they are on the front of a train it is quite another! To date, this is the most locos I have ever seen at the front of a train of any type. 66108, 66227, 66034, 66122 and 66200 approach Woking with 6Y42, the 09.02 Eastleigh Yard to Hoo Junction. Of these locos, 66108 is now on hire to DRS and repainted, 66227 is working in Poland, 66034 is now in DB red, 66122 is another with DRS and finally 66200 has not changed at all! 30 January 2009.

We now see a septet comprising of 66015, 66037, 66041, 66184, 66162, 66158 and 66117 approaching Salisbury with 0X12, the 10.53 Margam to Eastleigh convoy. This often ran as an 'X-ray' when formed of more than about five locos. As for these locos, all still currently work in the UK, but 66184 has since been sold to GBRf and now carries the number 66787, and 66162 is now blue as *Maritime Intermodal Five*. 23 February 2013.

Now we have an octuplet in the Avon Valley, near Bath, as 66154, 66200, 66132, 66053, 66198, 66148, 66005 and 66100 pass by as 0X12, the 10.53 Margam to Eastleigh convoy. It is always best to try and photograph this working before it reaches Westbury, as quite often all or some locos only go that far. All of these locos currently operate in the UK, but 66132 has become GBRf's 66785, 66148 is now in Maritime colours as *Maritime Intermodal Seven*, 66005 is also in blue and named *Maritime Intermodal One,* and 66100 is in DB red and carrying the name *Armistice 100*. 14 February 2015.

Each year some of the many RHTT trains that run throughout the autumn are worked by top and tail Class 66s. Here are just a few examples. This is 66017 and 66001 caked in dirt at Princes Risborough while working a 3J04 Chiltern Line circuit from Acton. 10 October 2011.

The West Country also sees DB activity on the RHTT circuit. This is 66027 and 66136 passing Totnes with the 3S56 10.00 St Blazey to St Blazey via Newton Abbot Hackney Yard, which was an extra working to the normal itinerary. 66136 is in its unique modified DB red livery with decals commemorating the first through train from China to the UK, while 66027 also now carries DB colours. 6 October 2017.

Heading south on the approach to Castle Cary, this is 66160 and 66082 with the usual 3J13, the 08.45 Westbury to St Blazey via Salisbury run. 66082 is now carrying DB red. 26 November 2010.

66152 and 66024 approach Bristol Temple Meads with the 3S59 23.18 Bristol Barton Hill to Bristol Barton Hill RHTT. In recent years, Colas Rail has operated this circuit, usually starting and finishing at Swindon. 29 November 2017.

To end this volume, we see three more shots of the St Blazey-based set. This is 3J13, the 08.50 Westbury to St Blazey, waiting to depart Salisbury after a short layover worked by 66116 and 66098. 15 October 2021.

Another shot of the same train as the previous image waiting to depart the bay platform at Salisbury.
15 October 2021.

Also working 3J13, the 08.50 Westbury to St Blazey, is 66074 and 66027 passing the famous section of line at Dawlish while heading west. Both of these locos are now in DB red. 27 October 2017.

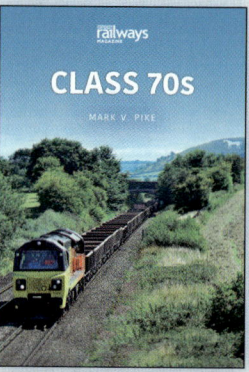
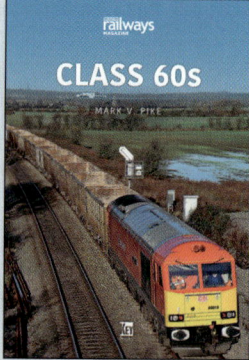
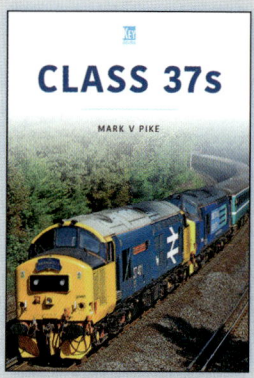

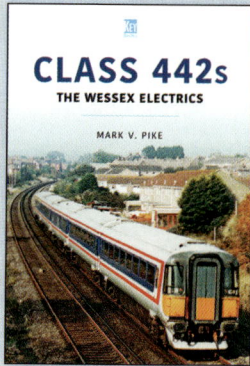